Vol 11

MAZE

Ages 4-6

FOR KIDS

MAZE BOOK

SOCIAL MEDIA

f /MySweetBooks1

🐦 /MySweetBooks1

📷 /MySweetBooks1

📌 /MySweetBooks

Email Us : mysweetbooks1@gmail.com

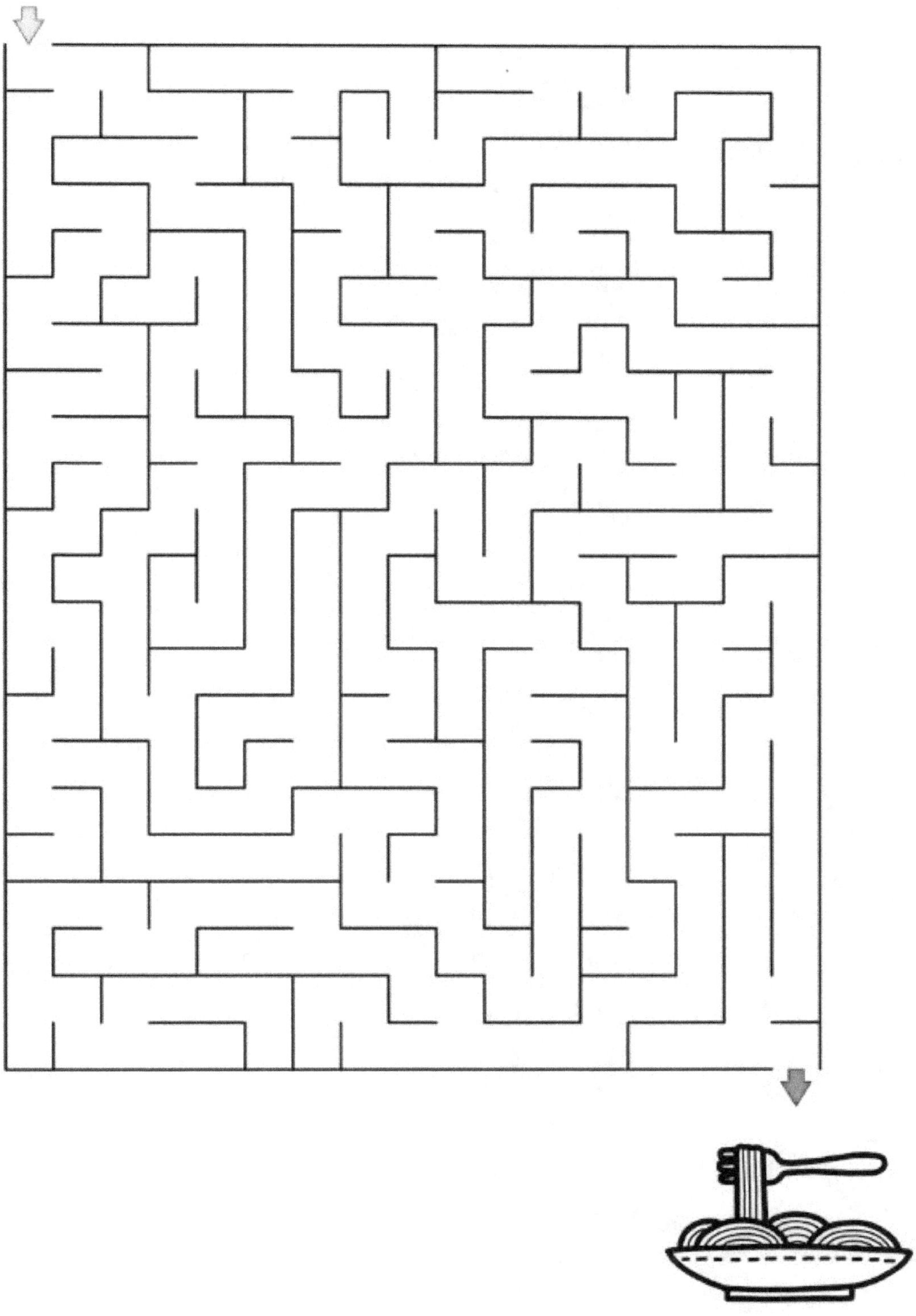

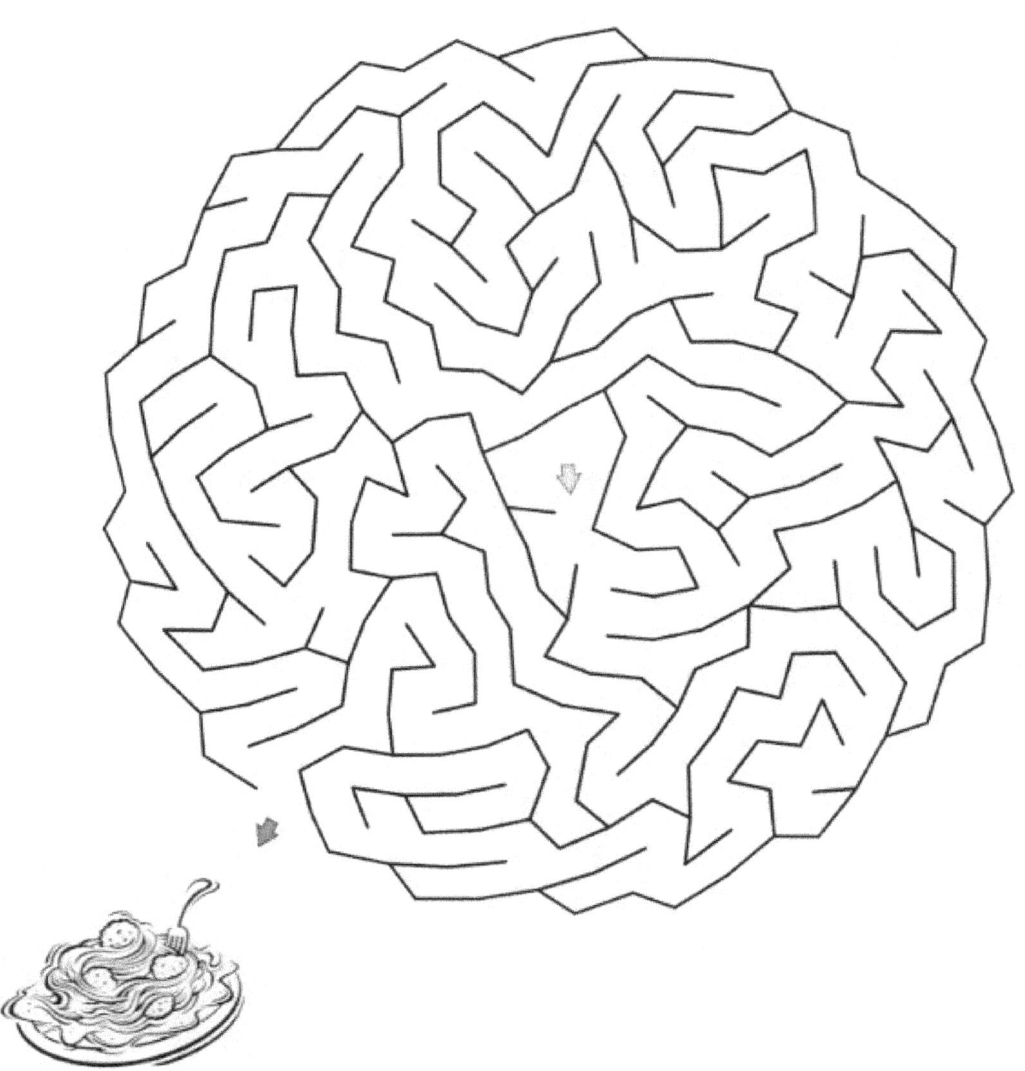

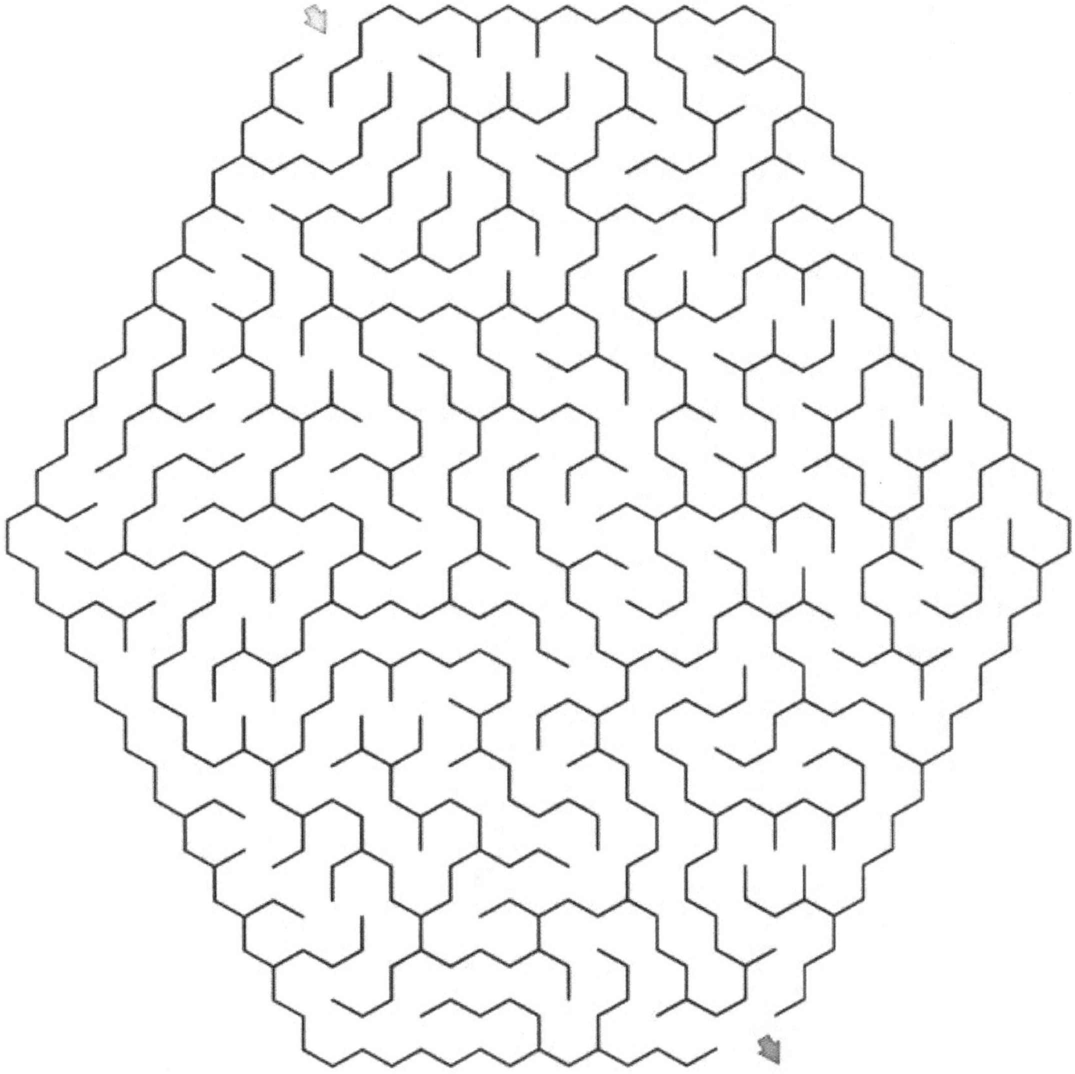

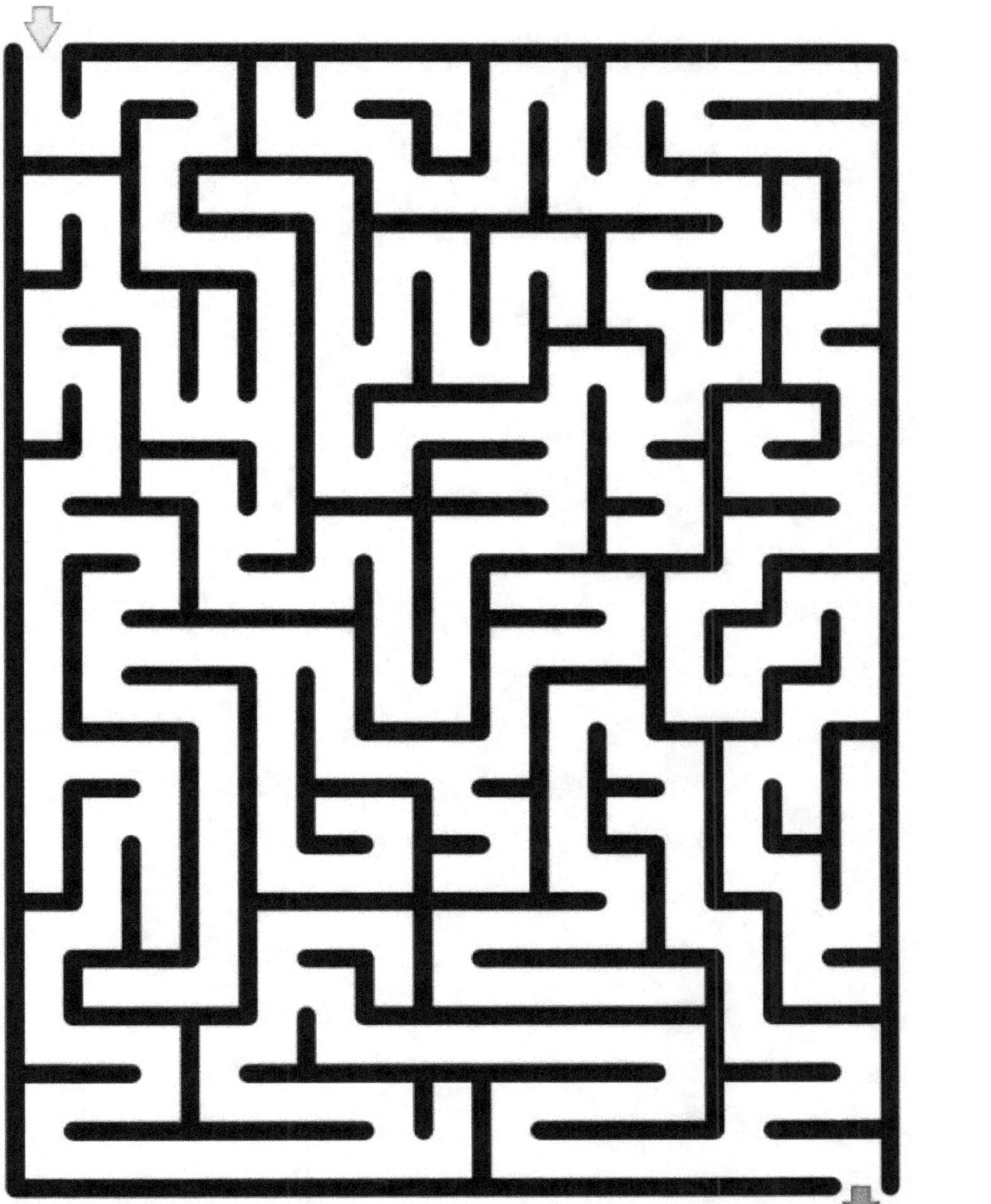

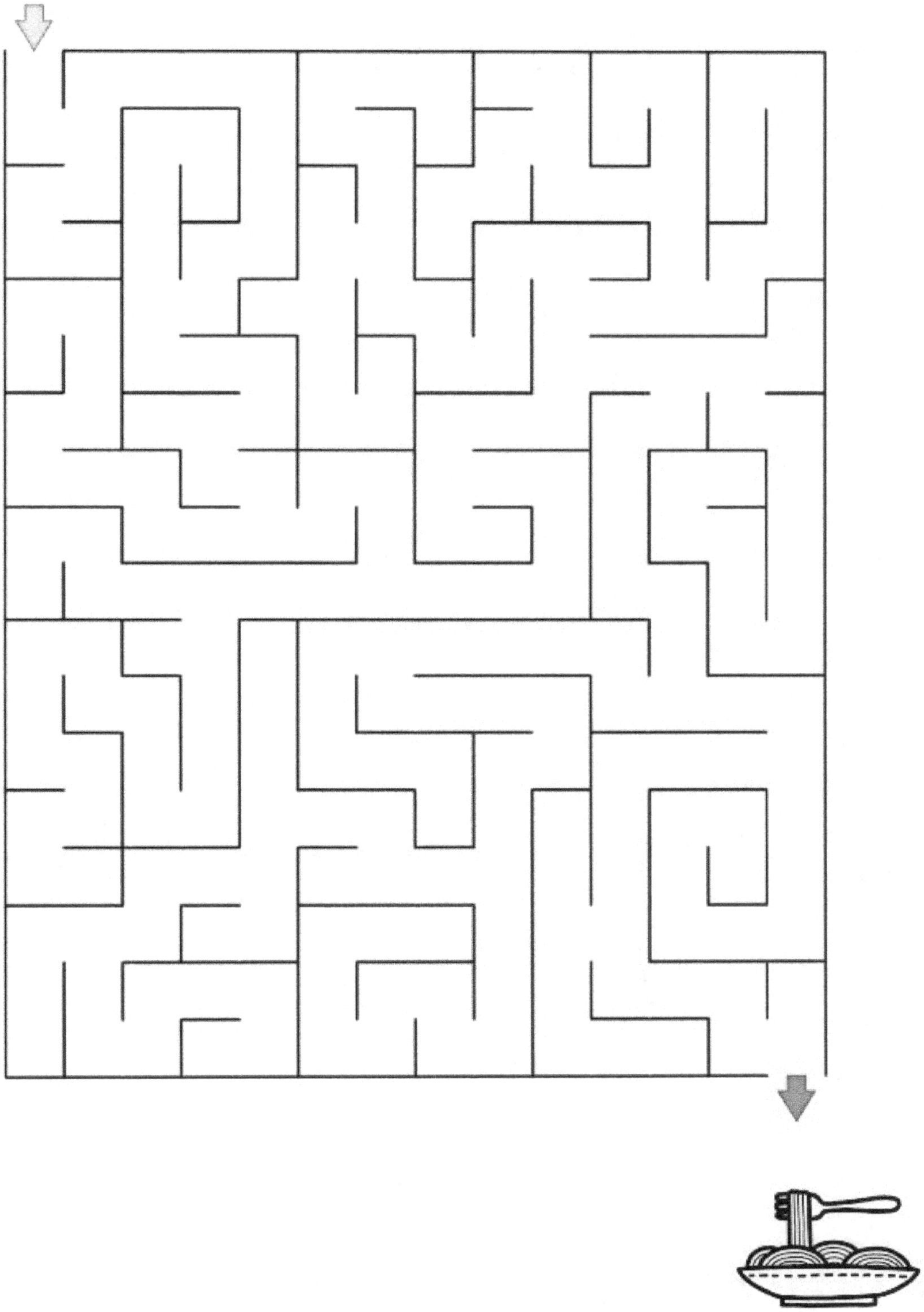

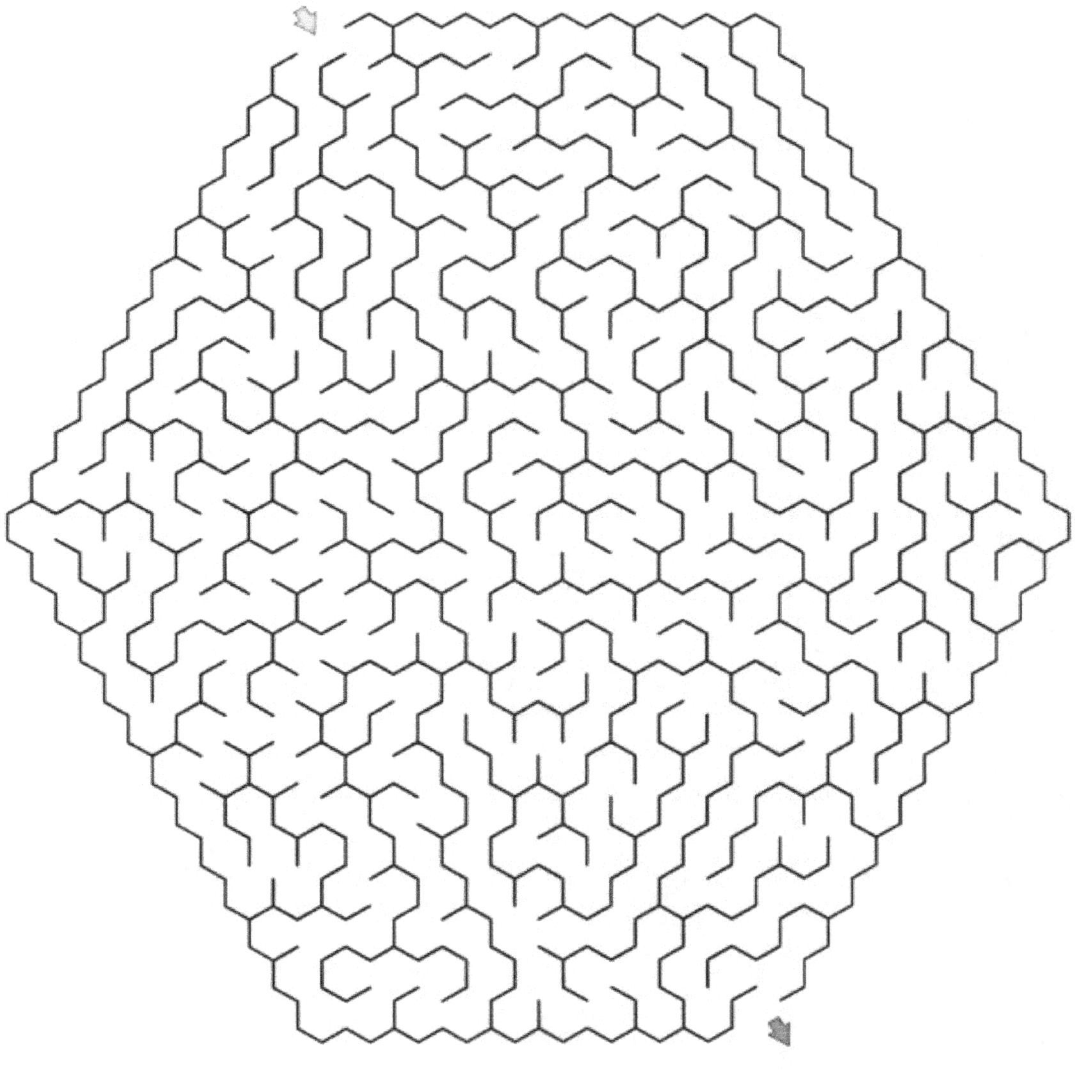

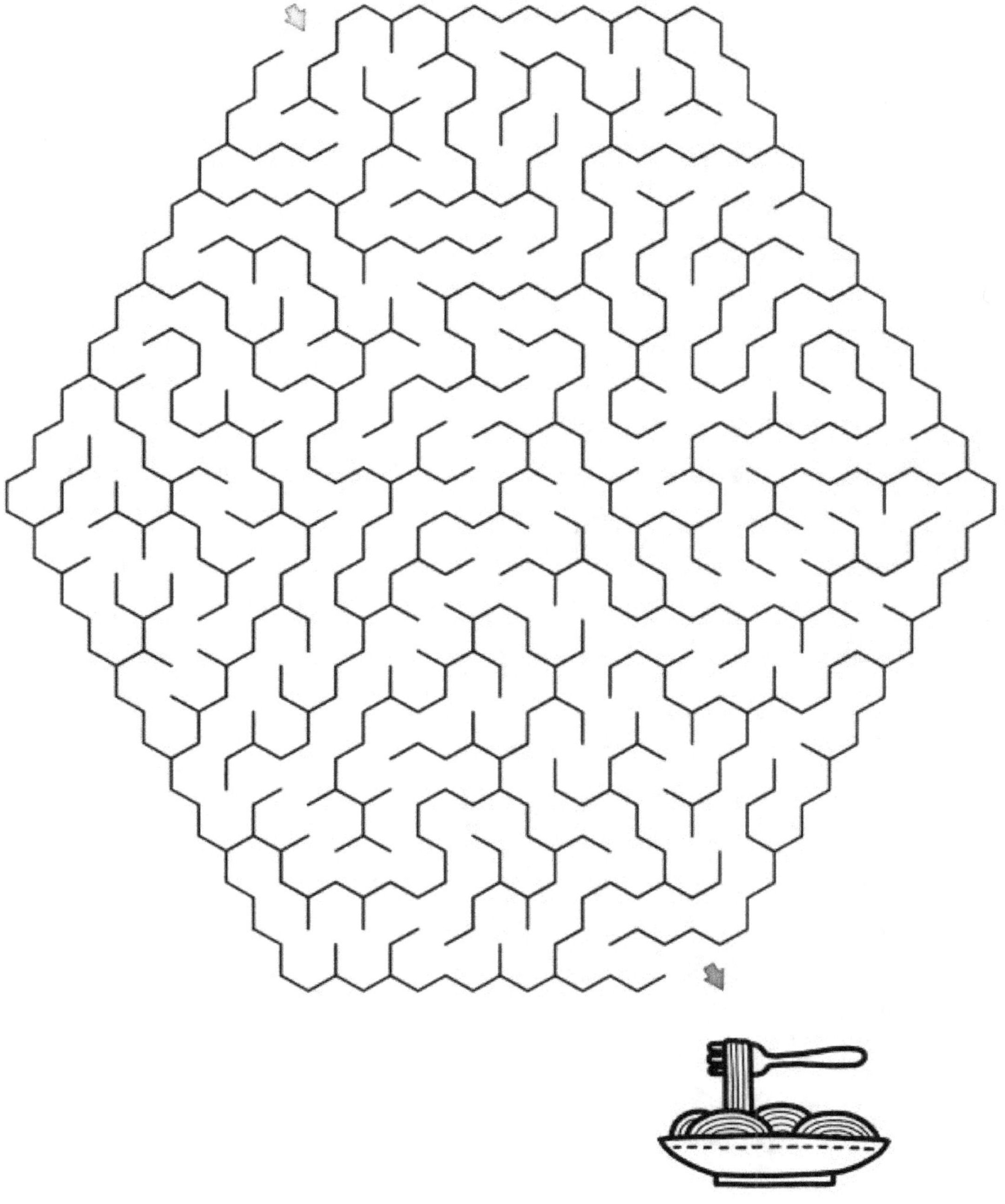

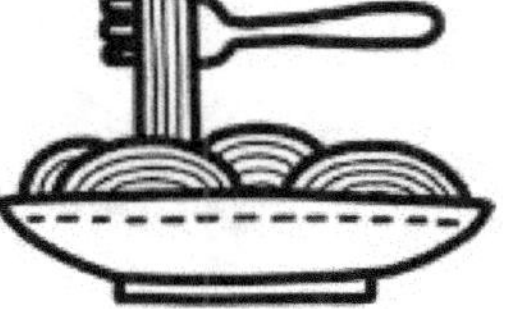

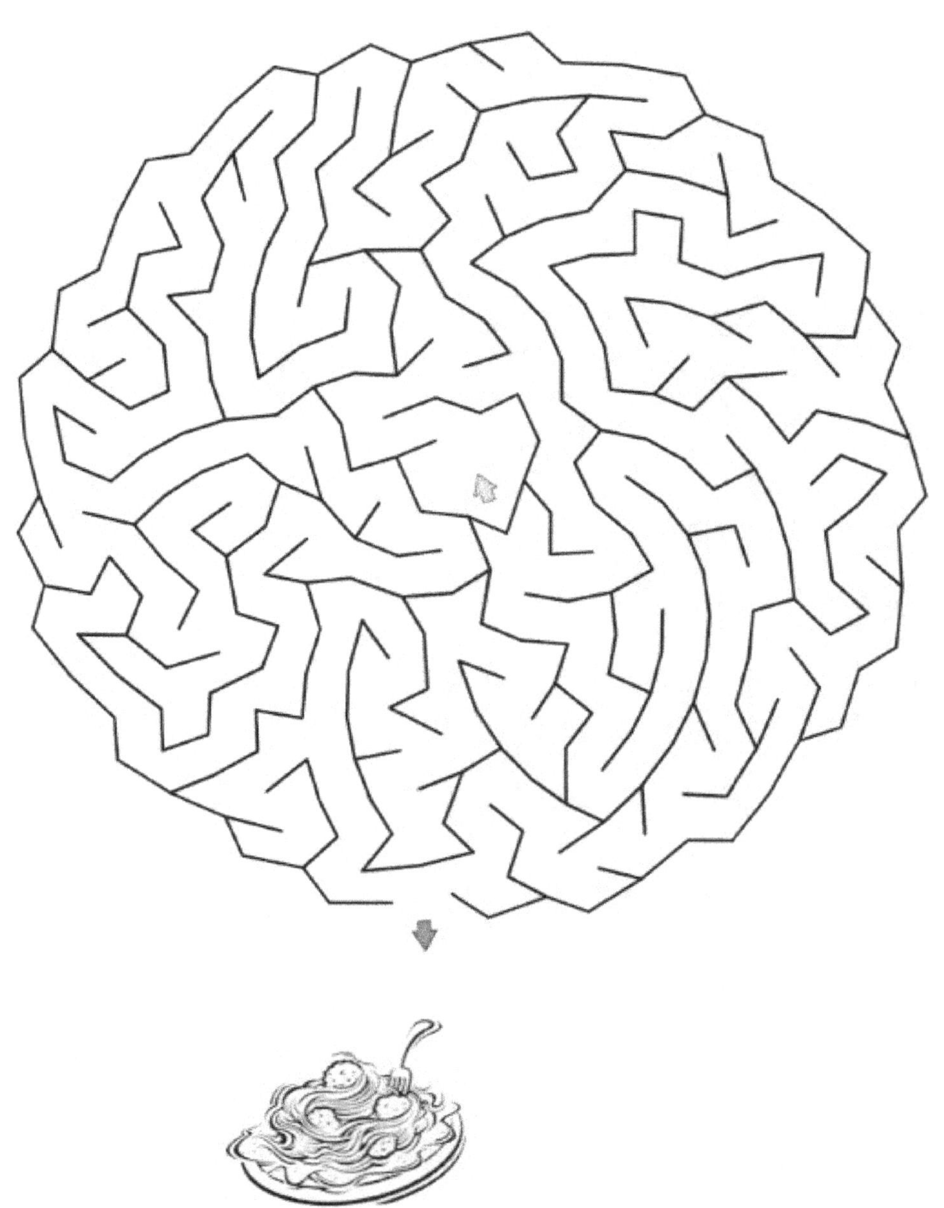

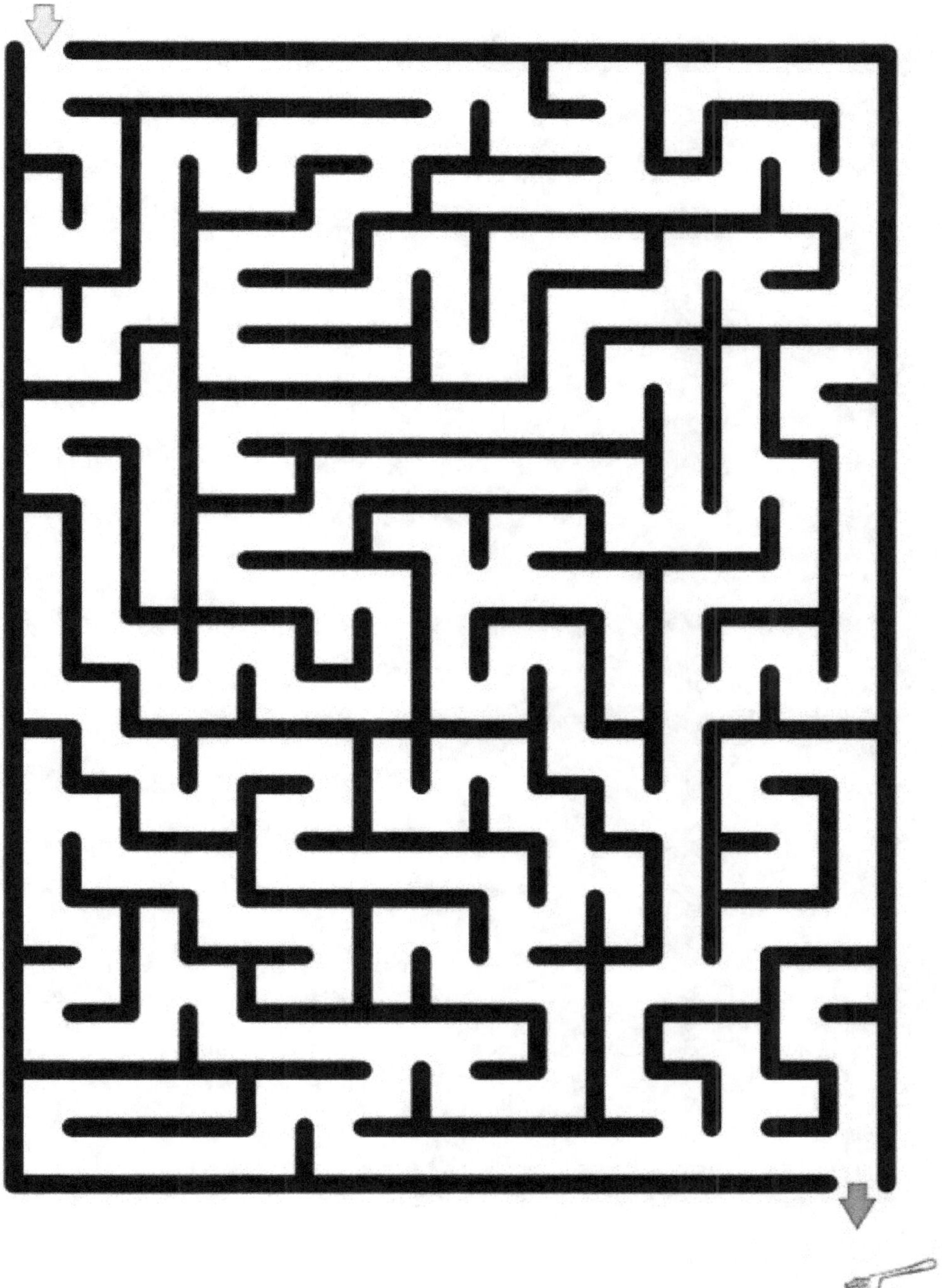

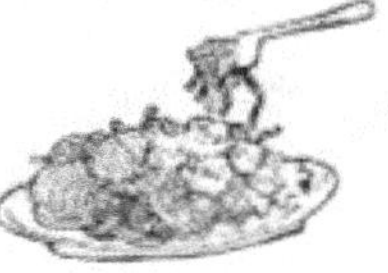

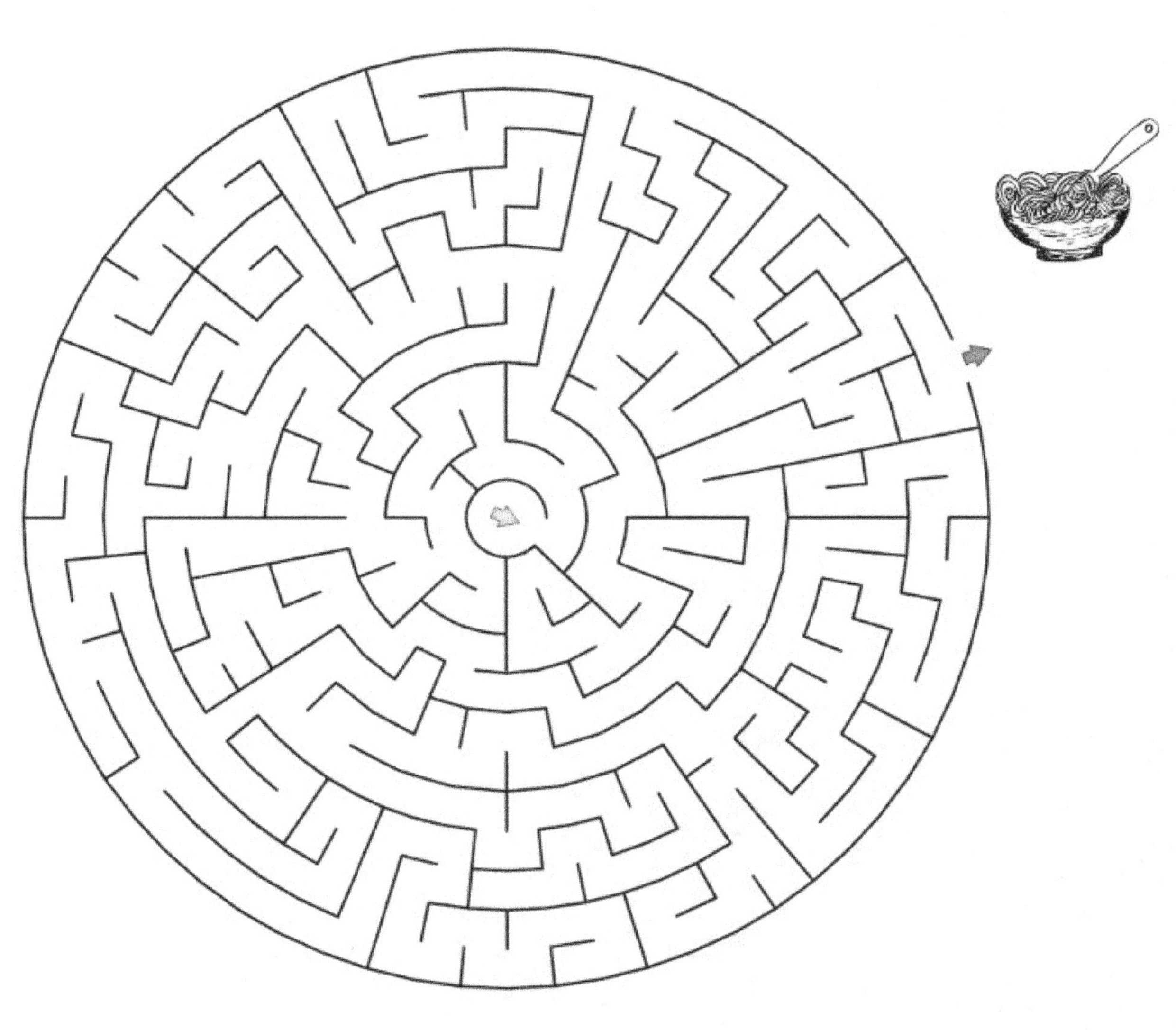

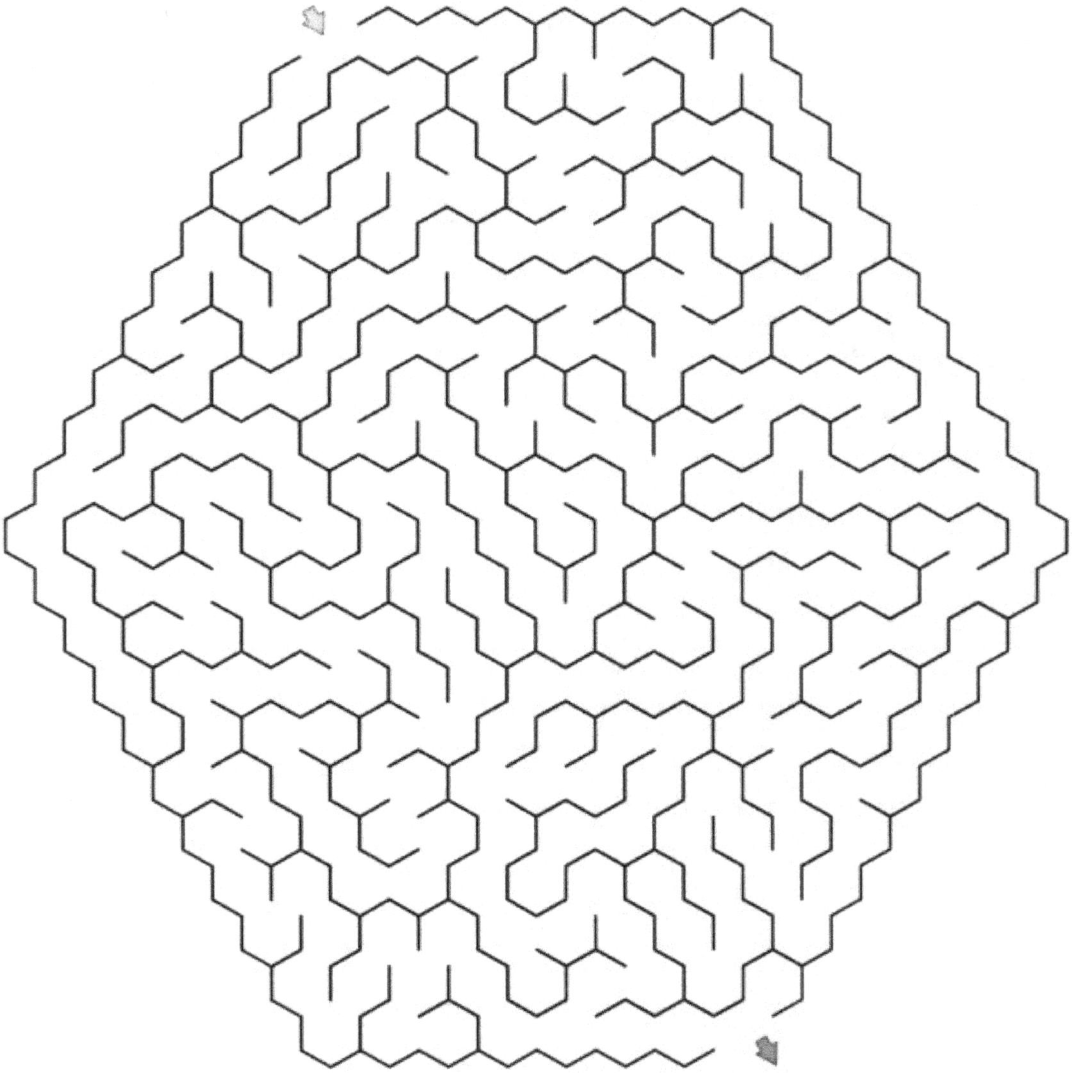

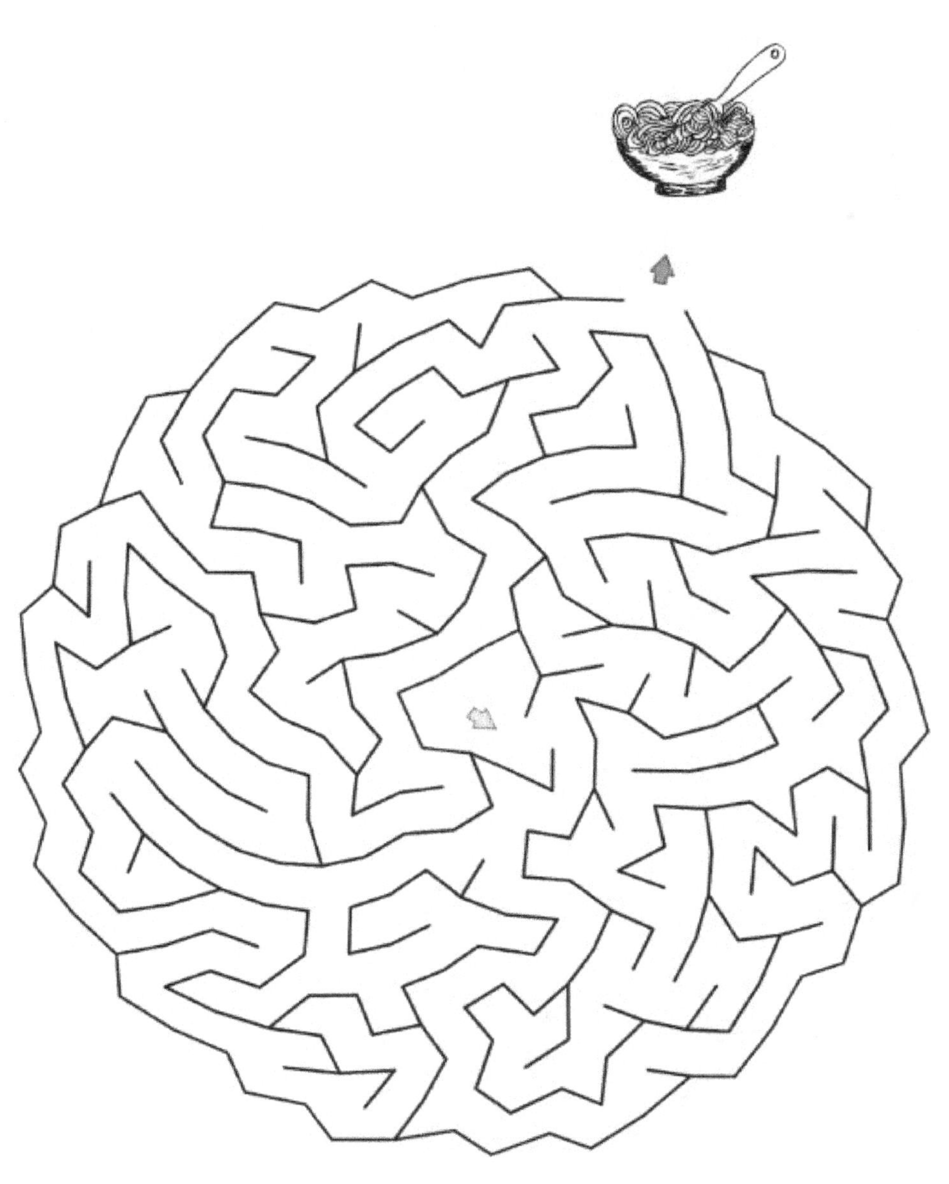